COLE:

THE NEXT BIG THING

Rising Stars Collection

By

RICHARD DEES

ISBN: 9798873882700

Imprint: Independently published

Printed in United Kingdom First Edition: January, 2024

Latest Edition: September, 2024

DEDICATION

To every young dreamer who has ever kicked a ball,
To the underdogs who rise, and those who stand tall.
To the fans, the families, the teams near and far,
This book is for you, wherever you are.
May you always find joy in the game's simple pleasure, And may your love for football be a treasure forever.

Richard Dees - Lifelong football fan

CONTENTS

COLE: THE NEXT BIG THING

Introduction: The Rise of a New Star

Step into the world of Cole Palmer, where dreams are crafted on the cracked pavements of Wythenshawe and realized on the grandest stages of world football. From the moment he first kicked a ball, it was clear Cole was destined for greatness. But his journey was far from easy; it was a path marked by hard work, resilience, and a relentless pursuit of excellence.

"Cole: The Next Big Thing" is not just a story about football; it's a story about believing in yourself, pushing past your limits, and turning your dreams into reality. Join Cole as he takes you through the highs and lows of his journey, from his early days in Manchester to his rise as one of England's brightest young talents.

CHAPTER 1: A DREAM BEGINS IN WYTHENSHAWE

It was a typically grey and drizzly afternoon in Wythenshawe, Manchester, the kind that makes the streets glisten with the sheen of recent rain. For most, it was just another day, but for seven-year-old Cole Palmer, it was another opportunity to hone his footballing skills. The cracked pavement outside his house, bordered by rows of tightly packed terraced homes, served as his first pitch—a humble stage where he would start his journey to greatness.

Cole's love for football was evident from the moment he could walk. Even as a toddler, he could be found chasing after a ball in the family's small living room, much to the amusement of his parents, Nicola and Shaun Palmer. Nicola, who worked as a teaching assistant, often remarked, "If he could've slept with a football, he would have!" She was the first to notice that Cole wasn't just playing—he was practicing, always trying to perfect his dribbles, always looking for the next move.

Shaun Palmer, a dedicated father and an ardent football fan, saw the potential in his son early on. Shaun had always been passionate about the game himself, and he was determined to support Cole's budding talent. "Football is a game of inches, Cole," Shaun would say as they practiced in the backyard, "You've got to be sharper, faster, and smarter than everyone else."

The backyard of their modest home quickly transformed into a makeshift training ground. Shaun set up small goals and used cones to create dribbling challenges, while Cole, with a look of intense concentration on his face, would weave through them, mastering the art of ball control. They would often play until dusk, the fading light the only thing that could pull Cole away from the game.

Despite his young age, Cole's natural talent was unmistakable. His ability to keep the ball close to his feet, his vision on the pitch, and his unyielding determination to improve set him apart from other kids his age. By the time he was four, he could juggle a football for what seemed like hours, often outlasting the local teenagers who gathered on the same streets to play.

Wythenshawe, a neighbourhood known for its

strong community spirit, was more than just a backdrop to Cole's early life; it was the place where his love for football was nurtured. The neighbourhood kids would often stop their games to watch Cole, the "little wizard," as they called him, showcase his skills. He wasn't just playing football; he was commanding it, even at such a tender age.

As Cole grew, his reputation in the local football scene began to spread. It wasn't long before he caught the attention of Fletcher Moss Rangers, a local football club with a strong history of developing young talent. At just eight years old, Cole joined the club's under-9 team, marking the first significant step in his footballing journey.

At Fletcher Moss Rangers, Cole's skills were quickly recognized by his coach, Dave Horrocks. "This lad has something special," Dave would often tell the other coaches. "He's got a touch that you can't teach, a natural flair that's rare at his age." Under Dave's guidance, Cole's abilities began to flourish. The training sessions were more structured than the impromptu games on the streets, but Cole thrived in this environment, always eager to learn and improve.

One particularly rainy Saturday, Fletcher Moss Rangers were playing a match against a strong local rival. The pitch was muddy, and the rain poured down relentlessly, making it difficult for most of the young players to control the ball. But not for Cole. He darted across the field with the ball seemingly glued to his feet, his small frame weaving through defenders as if they were mere obstacles in a training drill. That day, Cole scored a hat-trick, leading his team to a hard-fought victory.

After the game, as the team huddled together, drenched but elated, Dave put his arm around Cole. "You're going to go far, son," he said with a smile. "Just keep playing the way you did today, and there'll be no stopping you." These words stuck with Cole, fueling his desire to push himself even harder.

At home, the Palmer household was buzzing with pride. Nicola, ever the supportive mother, would often remind Cole to stay humble. "It's not just about winning, love," she'd say as she ruffled his hair, "It's about playing with heart and never forgetting where you come from."

Shaun, on the other hand, would discuss tactics with Cole at the dinner table, replaying moments from the game in his mind. "Remember that second goal?" Shaun would ask. "You didn't just beat those defenders, you out-thought them. That's what makes a great player."

As the years passed, Cole continued to shine at Fletcher Moss Rangers, and it became increasingly clear that he was destined for bigger things. Scouts from major clubs began to take notice, often attending his matches with growing interest. Despite the attention, Cole remained grounded, his focus always on the next game, the next goal, the next opportunity to improve.

In 2016, when Cole was just 14, an opportunity arose that would change his life. Manchester City, one of the biggest clubs in the world, invited him for a trial with their youth academy. The news came one evening after dinner, as Shaun casually mentioned it to Cole, trying to downplay the excitement in his voice. "Manchester City wants to see you play, Cole," he said, a grin spreading across his face.

For Cole, this was more than just a chance to play for a big club; it was the validation of all the hard work, all the early mornings and late nights spent practicing in the rain and cold. As he lay in bed that night, staring at the ceiling, he could hardly contain his excitement. He knew this was just the beginning of a new chapter, a bigger challenge, and he was ready for it.

The trial day arrived, and as Cole walked onto the pristine pitches of Manchester City's academy, he felt a mixture of nerves and excitement. But once the ball was at his feet, all the anxiety melted away. He played with the same freedom and joy he had always known, impressing the coaches with his vision, technique, and maturity beyond his years.

That evening, after what felt like an eternity, Cole received the news that he had been accepted into the academy. The Palmer family celebrated quietly at home, aware that while this was a huge step, the journey was just beginning.

Cole's move to Manchester City was the start of a new adventure, one that would take him from the streets of Wythenshawe to the grand stages of world football. But no matter where the game took him, Cole never forgot the place where it all began, the cracked pavements where he first fell in love with football, and the family who supported him every step of the way.

And so, the young boy from Wythenshawe began his ascent, one kick at a time, towards the top of the footballing world.

CHAPTER 2: SKY BLUE DREAMS

July 1, 2016, was a day that Cole Palmer would never forget. It was the day he officially joined Manchester City's elite academy, marking the beginning of a new chapter in his young life. For a boy who had spent countless hours playing football on the streets of Wythenshawe, stepping onto the manicured fields of one of the world's top football academies was nothing short of a dream come true. But with this dream came new challenges that would test Cole in ways he had never experienced before.

A New World

As Cole walked through the gates of the City Football Academy, he was awestruck by the state-of-the-art facilities. Everything was pristine—the pitches were perfectly maintained, the gym was filled with the latest equipment, and the walls were adorned with images of Manchester City legends. It was a world away from the muddy fields of Fletcher Moss Rangers. But amid the excitement,

Cole felt the weight of expectation pressing down on him. He knew that the journey ahead would be difficult, and that he would have to work harder than ever before to succeed.

The first few weeks at the academy were a whirlwind. The training se-ssions were intense, far more demanding than anything Cole had experienced before. The pace of play was faster, the physicality of the game was more pronounced, and the tactical instructions were complex. Cole quickly realized that he was no longer the best player on the pitch—everyone around him was equally talented, if not more so.

One particular training session stood out in Cole's memory. It was a drizzly Tuesday afternoon, and the team was practicing their passing drills. The coaches had set up a drill designed to improve quick decision-making and ball control under pressure. As the drill progressed, Cole found himself struggling to keep up. The other boys were quicker, their passes more precise. By the end of the session, Cole was exhausted and frustrated. He felt like he was falling behind.

Later that evening, as Cole sat alone in his room at the academy's residence, he couldn't shake the feeling of doubt creeping in. "What if I'm not good enough?" he thought to himself. But then, he remembered the words of his father, Shaun: "Football is a game of inches. You've got to be sharper, faster, and smarter than everyone else." Those words echoed in his mind, reigniting the fire within him. Cole knew that he couldn't give up— not now, not when he had come this far.

Overcoming Challenges

Determined to improve, Cole threw himself into his training. He spent extra hours in the gym, working on his strength and endurance to match the physical demands of the game. He also began studying the tactics of the game more closely, watching videos of professional matches and paying attention to how the best players moved and made decisions on the pitch. Slowly but surely, Cole started to adapt to the new level of play.

A turning point came during a training match a few months after he had joined the academy. The coaches had organized a friendly match against another top academy, and Cole was determined to make an impact. The match was intense, with both teams battling for control of the game. Cole, playing in his favored attacking midfield position, found himself in a one-on-one situation with the opposing team's defender.

The defender was much larger and more

experienced than Cole, but Cole remembered the countless hours he had spent practicing dribbling with his father in their backyard. He feinted to the right, then quickly shifted the ball to his left foot, leaving the defender wrong-footed. With a burst of speed, Cole darted past him and slotted the ball into the bottom corner of the net. The thrill of the goal surged through him—he had done it.

The coaches took notice of Cole's performance. "That's the kind of play we need to see more of," one of the coaches, Mark Burton, said after the match. "Keep that up, and you'll go far." It was the validation Cole needed, a sign that he was on the right track.

Dealing with Pressure

As the months passed, Cole continued to improve, but with progress came pressure. Being part of Manchester City's academy meant that every move he made was scrutinized. The expectations were sky-high—not just from the coaches, but from himself as well. He knew that only a select few would make it to the first team, and he was determined to be one of them.

One of the biggest challenges Cole faced was the mental pressure of being in such a competitive environment. The academy was filled with talented players, each one striving to be the best, and it was easy to get lost in the competition. But Cole knew that the key to success was not just in physical skill, but in mental resilience.

To cope with the pressure, Cole developed routines that helped him stay focused. Before every training session, he would spend a few minutes alone, visualizing himself on the pitch, making the perfect pass or scoring a goal. This mental preparation became a crucial part of his routine, allowing him to stay calm and composed even in the most intense situations.

His family also played a significant role in helping him manage the pressure. Nicola, his mother, was always just a phone call away, ready to offer words of encouragement whenever Cole felt overwhelmed. "Remember why you started, Cole," she would say. "You're doing this because you love it. Keep that in your heart, and you'll be fine."

Key Matches and Milestones

Cole's hard work began to pay off in tangible ways. One of the most memorable moments of his early academy career came during the 2017-18 season. Manchester City's Under-16s were playing in a tournament against some of the best youth teams in Europe. The pressure was immense, with scouts from top clubs watching every game.

In the semi-final match against Barcelona's famed La Masia academy, Cole had one of his best performances to date. The game was tied 1-1 with just minutes remaining. Cole received the ball just outside the penalty box, surrounded by defenders. With a quick drop of his shoulder, he created a small window of space and unleashed a curling shot that sailed into the top corner of the net, winning the game for his team.

The goal was a defining moment for Cole—it wasn't just a victory, but a statement that he could compete with the best. His performance earned him widespread praise, and from that moment on, he was seen as one of the brightest prospects in the academy.

A New Confidence

By the end of his second year at the academy, Cole had grown both as a player and as a person. He had faced the challenges of transitioning to a top club and had come out stronger on the other side. The doubts that had once plagued him were now replaced with a quiet confidence. He knew that the road ahead would still be tough, but he was ready for it.

As he prepared for the next stage of his journey, Cole often reflected on how far he had come. From the streets of Wythenshawe to the elite training grounds of Manchester City, he had taken each step with determination and heart. Now, with his dreams firmly in sight, Cole was ready to take on whatever challenges came next.

The sky blue of Manchester City had become more than just the color of his kit—it was the color of his dreams, dreams that were now within reach.

CHAPTER 3: KNOCKING ON THE DOOR

September 30, 2020, was a day that Cole Palmer had been working towards his entire life. After years of dedication, sweat, and countless hours on the training pitch, the moment had finally arrived—his first-team debut for Manchester City. The build-up to this day was intense, filled with nerves, excitement, and the weight of expectations. But for Cole, it was also a moment of pure joy—a culmination of all the hard work that had brought him to this point.

The Emotional Build-Up

The announcement came during a training session at the City Football Academy. As the players gathered around the tactics board, Pep Guardiola, the legendary manager of Manchester City, began to outline the strategy for their upcoming League Cup match against Burnley. The team was filled with experienced stars, but Guardiola was known for giving young talents a chance to shine. As he read through the team sheet,

Cole's heart skipped a beat when he heard his name.

"You'll be coming on in the second half, Cole," Guardiola said with a reassuring nod. "Stay calm, play your game, and most importantly, enjoy the moment."

Cole could hardly believe it. After years of dreaming, he was about to step onto the pitch as a member of Manchester City's senior squad. That evening, as he left the training ground, he called his parents, unable to contain his excitement.

"Mum, Dad, I'm in the squad for tomorrow," Cole said, his voice trembling with emotion.

"That's incredible, Cole! We knew you could do it!" Nicola exclaimed, her pride evident through the phone. Shaun, equally emotional, added, "Remember everything we've practiced, son. Play with your heart, and the rest will follow."

The next day, Cole arrived at the Etihad Stadium early. The air was thick with anticipation as the team bused to Burnley's Turf Moor stadium. The senior players, seasoned in such moments, offered words of encouragement. Fernandinho, the team's captain, placed a hand on Cole's shoulder and said, "You've earned this, Cole. Just play like you always do."

As the team prepared in the dressing room, Cole could feel his nerves building. The atmosphere was electric, and the reality of playing alongside some of the world's best footballers began to sink in. But when he put on the sky-blue jersey, the nerves began to dissipate, replaced by a sense of purpose.

The Debut

When the second half arrived, Guardiola gave Cole the nod. "You're going on for Mahrez," he said. "Show them what you've got."

As Cole stepped onto the pitch, the floodlights illuminating the field, he took a deep breath. This was it—the moment he had been waiting for. The noise of the crowd, the intensity of the game, it all seemed to fade away as he focused on the ball at his feet.

Burnley was known for its physical style of play, and the match had been a tough battle up until that point. But Cole, despite his inexperience at this level, didn't shy away. He immediately got involved, receiving the ball in midfield and linking up play with his teammates. His first touch was confident, and as the minutes passed, he began to find his rhythm.

A key moment came when Cole found himself in possession on the edge of Burnley's penalty area. He spotted a gap in the defense and threaded a delicate pass through to Ferran Torres, who came close to scoring. Although the goal didn't come, Guardiola nodded approvingly from the sidelines. It was clear that Cole belonged at this level.

The match ended in a 3-0 victory for Manchester City, and while Cole didn't get on the scoresheet, his debut was a success. In the dressing room after the game, the atmosphere was celebratory. "Well done, Cole," Guardiola said. "This is just the beginning."

The Reaction

When the final whistle blew, Cole couldn't help but smile. He had done it—he had played for Manchester City's first team. The pride he felt was overwhelming, but it was nothing compared to the joy in his parents' voices when he called them after the game.

"We're so proud of you, Cole!" Nicola said, her voice filled with emotion. "We knew you could do it, and we can't wait to see what comes next."

Shaun, ever the coach, added, "You played

brilliantly, son. Keep working hard, and there's no limit to what you can achieve."

The media also took notice. Reports praised Cole's composure and technical ability, noting that he had the potential to become a regular in the first team. For Cole, however, the most important thing was that he had taken the first step towards his dream of playing at the highest level.

UEFA Champions League Debut

Just a few weeks after his League Cup debut, another significant milestone came in Cole's career—his UEFA Champions League debut. On December 9, 2020, Manchester City was facing Marseille in the group stage of the competition. With City already through to the knockout rounds, Guardiola decided to give some of the younger players a chance to gain experience on the European stage.

As the team prepared in the dressing room, Guardiola approached Cole. "You're starting tonight," he said simply, handing him the match shirt with the iconic Champions League patch on the sleeve. The significance of the moment wasn't lost on Cole—this was the competition every young footballer dreamed of playing in.

That night, as the Champions League anthem played and the teams lined up on the pitch, Cole felt a surge of pride. He glanced up at the stands, empty due to the pandemic, but he knew his family was watching from home, cheering him on.

The match was intense, with Marseille fighting hard to salvage their campaign. Cole, playing on the right wing, was involved in several key plays. His most notable moment came in the second half when he received a cross-field pass from Raheem Sterling. Taking the ball down with a deft touch, Cole drove towards the Marseille defense before laying off a perfectly timed pass to Ilkay Gündogan, who nearly scored.

Manchester City won the match 3-0, and Cole's performance was widely praised. "To play in the Champions League is something special," Cole said in a post-match interview. "It's something I've always dreamed of, and to do it with this team is incredible."

His family was, as always, his biggest supporters. Shaun and Nicola stayed up late to talk to Cole after the game, their pride evident in every word. "You're living your dream, Cole," Nicola said. "And we're living it with you."

Staying in Guardiola's Plans

As the season progressed, Cole's consistent performances in training kept him firmly in Guardiola's plans. Guardiola, known for his meticulous approach to coaching, was impressed by Cole's dedication and willingness to learn. Despite being one of the youngest members of the squad, Cole was always one of the first on the training pitch and one of the last to leave.

During a tactical session one day, Guardiola took Cole aside. "You have the talent, Cole," he said, "but talent isn't enough. You need to be smart, to understand the game on a deeper level. Keep working hard, and you'll go far."

Cole took these words to heart. He continued to train with the same intensity, always seeking to improve. Whether it was working on his finishing, studying the movements of senior players, or refining his understanding of Guardiola's tactical philosophy, Cole was determined to make the most of every opportunity.

And those opportunities kept coming. By the end of the 2020-21 season, Cole had made several appearances in the Premier League, further cementing his place in the squad. For Cole, the journey was just beginning, but the foundation had been laid. He had knocked on the door, and now it was up to him to push it wide open.

As Cole reflected on his first season with the senior team, he knew that there was still a long way to go. But with each match, each training session, and each word of encouragement from his coaches and family, he felt more confident that he was on the right path. The dream that had started on the streets of Wythenshawe was becoming a reality, one step at a time.

CHAPTER 4: MAKING HIS MARK

The night of September 21, 2021, was one that Cole Palmer would remember for the rest of his life. The setting was the Etihad Stadium, where Manchester City was playing Wycombe Wanderers in the third round of the EFL Cup. For many, it was just another fixture in a long season, but for Cole, it was the night he would score his first senior goal for Manchester City—a moment that would forever be etched in his memory.

The Build-Up

The days leading up to the match were a whirlwind for Cole. After his promising debut the previous year and his consistent performances in training, Pep Guardiola had been keeping a close eye on the young midfielder. "You're doing well, Cole," Guardiola had told him after a particularly intense training session. "I think you're ready for more."

Cole had been included in the squad for the

Wycombe match, and this time, Guardiola hinted that he might get more than just a few minutes on the pitch. The anticipation was building, and as match day approached, Cole felt a mixture of excitement and nerves. "This could be my chance," he thought to himself, replaying the scenarios in his mind.

Match Day: The First Goal

The atmosphere at the Etihad Stadium that evening was electric. Although it was a midweek cup match against lower-league opposition, the City fans had turned out in force, eager to see their team in action. For Cole, stepping onto the pitch in front of thousands of cheering fans was both exhilarating and slightly intimidating. But as he looked around at the sea of sky-blue shirts, he reminded himself that this was what he had worked so hard for.

Guardiola had named a mix of experienced players and young talents in the starting lineup, and Cole was given a central role in midfield. As the match kicked off, City quickly took control of the game, dominating possession and probing Wycombe's defense.

The first half was a flurry of activity, with City creating numerous chances. Cole, playing with a freedom that belied his age, was at the heart of many of these moves, linking up play and driving forward with the ball. The crowd could sense that something special was brewing.

Then, in the 71st minute, the moment arrived. City was leading comfortably, and as the ball was played to Cole just outside the penalty area, the crowd's anticipation grew. Taking a quick touch to control the ball, Cole looked up and saw a gap in the defense. Without hesitation, he unleashed a powerful left-footed shot that curled past the outstretched arm of the Wycombe goalkeeper and into the bottom corner of the net.

For a split second, there was silence as the crowd processed what had just happened. Then, the stadium erupted in celebration. The roar of the fans was deafening as Cole sprinted towards the corner flag, arms outstretched in pure joy. His teammates quickly surrounded him, congratulating him with pats on the back and excited shouts. "What a goal, Cole!" one of them yelled, the excitement clear in his voice.

From the touchline, Guardiola clapped and smiled, clearly pleased with what he had just witnessed. "That's the Cole we know," he later said in the post-match interview. "He's got the quality and the confidence to make a difference in games like these."

The Reaction

After the match, which ended in a 6-1 victory for City, Cole could hardly contain his happiness. He had dreamed of this moment for years, and now it was finally real. As he made his way back to the dressing room, the fans continued to cheer, chanting his name—a sound that filled him with pride.

In the dressing room, the atmosphere was jubilant. The senior players, many of whom had taken him under their wing, were quick to offer their congratulations. "Great strike, Cole!" said Kevin De Bruyne, one of the team's leaders. "Keep playing like that, and you'll be scoring many more."

Fernandinho, the captain, was also full of praise. "You've got a bright future ahead of you," he said, his voice steady and reassuring. "Stay focused, keep working hard, and the sky's the limit."

That night, Cole called his parents, who had been watching the match from home. "I did it, Mum! I scored!" he exclaimed, the excitement still evident in his voice.

"We're so proud of you, Cole," Nicola replied,

her voice choked with emotion. "You've worked so hard for this, and it's just the beginning."

Shaun, ever the football enthusiast, added, "That was a brilliant goal, son. Just keep doing what you're doing, and you'll be unstoppable."

The Champions League Goal

As the season progressed, Cole continued to impress both in training and during the minutes he was given on the pitch. But it was his performance in the UEFA Champions League that truly marked his arrival on the European stage.

On October 19, 2021, Manchester City faced Club Brugge in a crucial group stage match. With City already leading 4-1, Guardiola decided to bring on Cole for the final minutes of the game, giving him another chance to showcase his talent on one of the biggest stages in football.

The match was already won, but Cole wasn't content to just see out the game. In the 67th minute, he found himself in possession of the ball just outside the Brugge penalty area. With defenders closing in, Cole executed a perfect one-two with Riyad Mahrez, creating just enough space to unleash a shot. The ball rocketed into the top corner of the net, leaving the goalkeeper with no chance.

The reaction from the City bench was immediate—players and staff alike leapt to their feet in celebration. Guardiola, who rarely showed much emotion on the sidelines, punched the air in delight. "That's what I'm talking about!" he shouted to his assistants.

For Cole, scoring in the Champions League was a dream come true. As he celebrated with his teammates, the significance of the moment began to sink in. He had not only scored for Manchester City; he had done it in one of the most prestigious competitions in world football.

The media quickly picked up on Cole's performance, with headlines praising the young midfielder's maturity and skill. "Palmer shines in City's European rout," read one article, while another declared, "The future is bright for Manchester City's latest star."

The Impact

Cole's Champions League goal had a profound impact on his career trajectory. It wasn't just the goal itself that mattered, but what it represented—a young player stepping up on the biggest stage and delivering when it counted. For Guardiola, it was further proof that Cole was ready for more responsibility.

In the weeks that followed, Cole found himself increasingly involved in the first-team setup. He was no longer just a promising youngster; he was a player who could make a difference, whether it was in the Premier League, the FA Cup, or the Champions League.

Reflecting on his journey, Cole knew that he had come a long way from the streets of Wythenshawe. But he also knew that this was just the beginning. There were still challenges ahead, still goals to be scored, and still dreams to be fulfilled. But with each match, each goal, and each word of encouragement from his coaches and teammates, Cole felt more certain than ever that he was on the right path.

And so, with his first goal for Manchester City and his stunning strike in the Champions League, Cole Palmer had well and truly made his mark.

CHAPTER 5: DREAMING BIG

The 2022-2023 season was one that Manchester City fans would remember for a long time, and for Cole Palmer, it was a season that would forever be etched in his memory as a pivotal period in his career. It was the season when Manchester City achieved an incredible treble—winning the Premier League, the FA Cup, and the UEFA Champions League. For Cole, playing a role in such an extraordinary achievement was both a dream come true and a learning experience that would shape the rest of his career.

The Premier League: Rising to the Challenge

As the 2022-2023 Premier League season kicked off, Manchester City was once again considered one of the favorites to win the title. The squad was packed with world-class talent, and the competition within the team was fierce. For Cole, this meant that every training session, every minute on the pitch, was an opportunity to prove himself.

Under Pep Guardiola's meticulous guidance, Cole continued to develop his game. His versatility allowed him to be deployed in various positions, whether in midfield or on the wing, and he was increasingly trusted to contribute in key moments.

One such moment came in a crucial match against Arsenal in February 2023. With the title race heating up, City needed a win to keep their momentum going. The match was tight, with both teams battling hard for control. In the 70th minute, Guardiola turned to Cole on the bench. "Get ready, Cole. We need your energy out there," he said, his voice calm but firm.

Cole entered the game with a determination that had become his hallmark. Within minutes, he made an impact, driving at the Arsenal defense with his quick feet and sharp movement. In the 82nd minute, he found himself in space on the edge of the box. Receiving a pass from Kevin De Bruyne, Cole took a quick touch and curled a shot towards the far post. The ball sailed past the Arsenal goalkeeper and into the net, sending the Etihad Stadium into raptures.

The goal proved to be the winner, and City's victory kept them at the top of the table. After the match, Guardiola praised Cole's contribution. "He's a special talent," Guardiola said in the post-match interview. "He understands the game at a high level, and tonight he showed that he can make a difference."

As the season progressed, City's consistency saw them pull ahead in the title race. Cole continued to play his part, coming off the bench in key games and starting in others, always delivering when called upon. When the final whistle blew on the last day of the season, City was crowned Premier League champions once again, and Cole had his first Premier League winner's medal.

The FA Cup: A Moment of Glory

The FA Cup had always been a competition that Cole admired. Growing up, he had watched countless finals on TV, dreaming of the day he might get to play in one. That dream became a reality on June 3, 2023, when Manchester City faced Manchester United in the FA Cup final at Wembley Stadium.

The build-up to the match was intense. It was a Manchester derby, and the stakes were higher than ever. For City, winning the FA Cup would bring them one step closer to the treble. For Cole, it was an opportunity to make his mark on one of the biggest stages in football.

As the team prepared in the dressing room, the atmosphere was a mix of focus and anticipation. Guardiola, as always, delivered his tactical instructions with precision. "Stay calm, stay focused, and play with the intensity we've shown all season," he said. Then, turning to Cole, he added, "This is your moment, Cole. Go out there and make it count."

The match was fiercely contested, with both teams pushing hard for an early advantage. City took the lead through a stunning volley from Ilkay Gündogan, but United quickly equalized. The tension was palpable as the game hung in the balance.

In the second half, with the score tied at 1-1, Guardiola brought Cole into the game. The young midfielder immediately set about making an impact, driving forward with purpose and linking up play with his teammates. Then, in the 77th minute, City won a free kick just outside the United penalty area.

As the players lined up, Cole positioned himself near the edge of the box, ready to pounce on any loose ball. Gündogan's free kick was blocked by the wall, but the ball bounced out to Cole, who struck it first-time with his left foot. The shot was low and hard, skimming through a crowd of players before finding the bottom corner of the net.

The City fans erupted in celebration as Cole ran towards the corner flag, arms outstretched, a look of pure joy on his face. The goal proved to be the winner, and City lifted the FA Cup, with Cole playing a pivotal role in the victory.

The UEFA Champions League: Reaching the Pinnacle

If the Premier League and FA Cup victories were special, winning the UEFA Champions League was the pinnacle. For Manchester City, it was the one trophy that had eluded them, and for Cole, playing in Europe's premier competition was the realization of a lifelong dream.

City's journey to the final was marked by some incredible performances, with Cole playing his part in several key matches. His versatility and tactical awareness made him a valuable asset in Guardiola's squad, and he was increasingly relied upon to provide energy and creativity in the latter stages of games.

The final, held in Istanbul on June 10, 2023, was against Inter Milan. The match was a tense affair, with both teams creating chances but struggling to break the deadlock. As the game entered the final

15 minutes, with the score still 0-0, Guardiola once again turned to Cole.

"Go out there and give us that spark, Cole," he said, his voice steady but filled with belief.

Cole entered the pitch with a sense of purpose. He knew the significance of the moment—not just for himself, but for the club and the fans. His presence immediately lifted the team, and City began to press harder for the winning goal.

In the 85th minute, City won a corner. As the ball was whipped in, it was partially cleared by the Inter defense, only to fall to Cole at the edge of the box. Without a moment's hesitation, he volleyed the ball back into the crowded area. It deflected off a defender and fell to Ruben Dias, who headed it into the net.

The stadium erupted as City took the lead. Cole's contribution had been crucial, and as the final whistle blew, securing City's first-ever Champions League title, he was engulfed by his teammates in a sea of celebration.

The UEFA Super Cup: A New Chapter

Just weeks after their historic Champions League triumph, City faced Sevilla in the UEFA Super

Cup, a match that would see the winners of the Champions League and the Europa League go head-to-head. For Cole, it was another chance to add to his growing list of honors.

The match, held on August 16, 2023, was played in Athens, and once again, City found themselves in a closely contested battle. The game was tied 1-1 as it headed into the final minutes, and Guardiola decided to bring on Cole, hoping his energy could tip the balance in City's favor.

As he took to the pitch, Cole could feel the weight of expectation. The match was being watched by millions around the world, and the pressure to perform was immense. But as always, Cole thrived under pressure.

In the 89th minute, City won a free kick in a dangerous position. As the ball was floated into the box, Cole made a late run towards the far post. The ball fell perfectly for him, and with a composed finish, he guided it past the Sevilla goalkeeper and into the net.

The goal proved to be the match-winner, and City lifted the UEFA Super Cup. For Cole, it was another step in his journey—a journey that had taken him from the streets of Wythenshawe to the grandest stages in world football.

Reflections on a Remarkable Season

As the 2022-2023 season came to a close, Cole took some time to reflect on what had been an extraordinary year. He had played a role in Manchester City's historic treble, scored crucial goals in some of the biggest matches of the season, and continued to grow as a player under the guidance of one of the world's greatest managers.

In interviews, Cole often spoke about the influence of his teammates and coaches. "Playing alongside players like Kevin De Bruyne and learning from Pep Guardiola has been incredible," he said. "Every day in training, I'm learning something new. The standards here are so high, and it pushes you to be the best version of yourself."

But for Cole, the most important lesson from the season was the value of hard work and perseverance. "There were times when it was tough, when the competition was fierce, and when the pressure was high," he reflected. "But I always believed in myself, and I always gave everything I had. This season has shown me that if you dream big and work hard, anything is possible."

As he looked ahead to the future, Cole knew that there were still many challenges to come. But with a Premier League title, an FA Cup, a Champions League, and a UEFA Super Cup already in his trophy cabinet, he was ready for whatever came next. The journey was far from over, and Cole Palmer was just getting started.

CHAPTER 6: SKY BLUE THROUGH AND THROUGH

As the dust settled on Manchester City's historic treble-winning season, Cole Palmer found himself at a pivotal point in his career. The triumphs of the 2022-2023 season had elevated him from a promising youngster to a player who had proven his worth on the biggest stages in football. But for Cole, the journey with Manchester City was not just about winning trophies—it was about learning, growing, and becoming an integral part of a club that he had come to love deeply.

A Strong Start to the New Season

The start of the 2023-2024 season brought new challenges and opportunities. Fresh off their treble success, Manchester City was now the team to beat, with every club in England and Europe eager to dethrone them. For Cole, this meant that the pressure to perform was higher than ever, but it was a challenge he welcomed with open arms.

In the opening match of the season, the Community Shield against Arsenal, Cole was brought on as a substitute. City had taken the lead through a stunning goal, but Arsenal equalized in the dying moments, sending the game to penalties. While City ultimately lost in the shootout, Cole's performance caught the eye of fans and pundits alike. He played with confidence, linking up well with his teammates and showing that he was ready to take on more responsibility.

Reflecting on the match, Cole later said, "It was disappointing to lose, but the most important thing is how we bounce back. We've got a long season ahead, and we're focused on building on what we achieved last year."

The UEFA Super Cup: A Moment of Redemption

Just days after the Community Shield, Manchester City traveled to Athens to face Sevilla in the UEFA Super Cup. For Cole, this match was not just about adding another trophy to his collection—it was about proving that he could deliver in the most important moments.

The match was tense, with both teams battling for supremacy. City took the lead, but Sevilla fought back to level the score. As the game moved into the final minutes, Guardiola turned to Cole, who had been warming up on the sidelines. "Go out there and make a difference, Cole," he said, his voice calm but filled with belief.

Cole entered the fray with a determination that had become his trademark. He immediately began to influence the game, using his quick feet and sharp passing to create opportunities. Then, in the 89th minute, came the moment of redemption. As City won a free kick on the left wing, Cole positioned himself near the far post, ready to pounce on any loose ball. The cross came in, and after a scramble in the box, the ball fell to Cole. With a composed finish, he slotted it past the goalkeeper, securing the victory for City.

The stadium erupted in celebration as Cole was mobbed by his teammates. It was a moment of pure joy, a reminder of why he loved the game. "That goal meant everything to me," Cole said after the match. "Winning the Super Cup was special, but being able to contribute in such an important way was even more rewarding."

Growing Under Guardiola's Guidance

Throughout the early months of the season, Cole's role in the team continued to grow. Guardiola, known for his ability to develop young talent, placed increasing trust in Cole, often turning to him in crucial moments. Whether starting or coming off the bench, Cole always delivered, playing with a maturity that belied his years.

In a Champions League group stage match against RB Leipzig, Cole was once again in the spotlight. City needed a win to secure their place in the knockout stages, and Guardiola decided to start Cole in a forward role. The match was tightly contested, but Cole's energy and creativity proved to be the difference. In the 67th minute, he picked up the ball just outside the box, dribbled past two defenders, and fired a low shot into the bottom corner. The goal was his second in the Champions League, and it helped City secure a 2-1 victory.

After the match, Guardiola was full of praise for his young star. "Cole has shown time and time again that he belongs at this level," the manager said. "His work ethic, his intelligence on the pitch, and his ability to stay calm under pressure are what make him such a special player."

Cole's teammates also recognized his growing influence. Kevin De Bruyne, one of City's leaders, took Cole aside after the Leipzig match. "You're doing brilliantly, Cole," De Bruyne said. "Just keep playing your game, and you'll go far."

A Season of Learning and Growth

As the 2023-2024 season progressed, Cole continued to develop, both as a player and as a person. The lessons he learned from playing alongside world-class talent were invaluable. Training with the likes of De Bruyne, Ilkay Gündogan, and Bernardo Silva every day pushed Cole to constantly improve his game. He studied their movements, their decision-making, and their understanding of the game, absorbing everything he could.

But it wasn't just about learning from others—Cole was also carving out his own identity as a player. His versatility allowed him to play in various positions, and his ability to read the game made him a key asset in Guardiola's tactical plans. Whether he was playing as a winger, a central midfielder, or even as a false nine, Cole always found a way to contribute.

Off the pitch, Cole remained grounded, never losing sight of where he had come from. The values instilled in him by his family—the importance of hard work, humility, and staying true to oneself— were always at the forefront of his mind. He knew that his success was the result of years of dedication and sacrifice, and he was determined to make the most of the opportunities he had been given.

Looking to the Future

As the season headed into its final stretch, Cole reflected on his journey so far. The treble-winning season had been a dream come true, but he knew that there was still much more to achieve. He was driven by a desire to keep improving, to keep pushing the boundaries of what he could accomplish.

"Playing for Manchester City is a privilege," Cole said in an interview. "I've learned so much from the players and coaches here, and I know that I still have a lot of growing to do. My goal is to keep working hard and to keep contributing to the team's success."

For Cole Palmer, the sky-blue jersey of Manchester City was more than just a uniform—it was a symbol of his journey, of the dreams he had chased since he was a young boy in Wythenshawe. As he looked ahead to the future, one thing was clear: Cole was ready to take on whatever challenges came his way, and he was determined to continue making his mark in the world of football.

CHAPTER 7: THREE LIONS PRIDE

Wearing the white shirt of England was a dream that Cole Palmer had nurtured since he was a young boy kicking a ball around the streets of Wythenshawe. From the moment he first laced up his boots, Cole imagined himself one day representing his country on the biggest stages in football. That dream began to take shape as he progressed through the youth ranks of England's national teams, leading to his senior debut and eventual participation in Euro 2024.

Early Days with England: A Journey Through the Youth Ranks

Cole's journey with England began long before his senior debut. As a talented youngster at Manchester City, he quickly caught the attention of England's youth scouts. His first taste of international football came when he was selected for the England Under-15 team, where he immediately stood out with his technical skills and footballing intelligence.

As Cole moved up the age groups, he continued to impress. His time with the England Under-17 team was particularly significant, as it gave him the opportunity to test himself against some of the best young players in the world. The highlight of this period came in 2019, when Cole was part of the squad that competed in the UEFA Under-17 European Championship. Although England didn't win the tournament, Cole's performances were a bright spot, earning him praise from coaches and teammates alike.

"Cole has a natural ability to read the game," said one of his youth coaches at the time. "He's got that special something that you can't teach. Watching him play, you know he's destined for big things."

These experiences at the youth level were crucial for Cole's development. The international stage brought new challenges—faster, more physical opponents, different styles of play, and the pressure of representing his country. But Cole thrived under these conditions, using each match as an opportunity to learn and grow.

In 2021, Cole's progress was rewarded when he was called up to the England Under-21 team. This was a significant step up, as the Under-21 level is seen as the final proving ground before making the leap to the senior team. Cole made his debut for the Under-21s in a European Championship qualifier against Kosovo, where he scored his first goal for the team, a well-taken finish that showcased his composure in front of goal.

The UEFA Under-21 European Championship: A Taste of Glory

The pinnacle of Cole's youth international career came in 2023 when he played a key role in England's triumphant campaign at the UEFA Under-21 European Championship. The tournament, held in Romania and Georgia, saw England face some of Europe's strongest teams, and Cole was at the heart of the action.

Throughout the group stages, Cole's performances were consistently impressive. He was a creative force in midfield, linking up play, creating chances, and scoring crucial goals. His ability to take on defenders and deliver pinpoint crosses made him one of England's standout players.

In the semi-final against Portugal, Cole delivered one of his best performances of the tournament. The match was tightly contested, with both teams creating chances but struggling to find the breakthrough. In the 75th minute, with the score still level, Cole received the ball on the edge of the box. With a quick drop of the shoulder, he beat his marker and unleashed a curling shot that flew into the top corner. The goal proved to be the winner, sending England into the final.

The final, against Germany, was another tense affair. Both teams played with caution, aware of the stakes. Once again, Cole was instrumental, his movement and passing opening up spaces in the German defense. While he didn't score in the final, his contributions were vital as England emerged victorious, lifting the trophy for the first time since 1984.

The victory was a moment of immense pride for Cole. Standing on the podium with his teammates, medal around his neck, and the trophy in hand, he felt a deep sense of accomplishment. "This is what you dream about as a kid," Cole said in an interview after the final. "Winning with England, representing your country—it doesn't get better than this."

Senior England Debut: A New Chapter Begins

Cole's performances for the Under-21s did not go unnoticed. In November 2023, his hard work and dedication paid off when he received his first call-up to the senior England squad. The moment he had been dreaming of for so long had finally arrived.

The call came while Cole was at Manchester City's training ground. As he checked his phone during a break, he saw the notification from the Football Association. "Congratulations, Cole Palmer. You've been selected for the England senior squad." His heart raced as he read the message, barely able to contain his excitement.

"Mum, Dad, you won't believe this—I've been called up to the England senior team!" he exclaimed when he called his parents.

"That's incredible, Cole!" Nicola responded, her voice filled with pride. "You've worked so hard for this. We're so proud of you."

Cole's senior debut came on November 17, 2023, in a friendly match against Malta at Wembley Stadium. As he stepped onto the hallowed turf, wearing the famous white shirt, the roar of the crowd sent shivers down his spine. This was it—he was playing for England, fulfilling the dream he had held onto for so many years.

The match itself was a comfortable 2-0 victory for England, with Cole coming on as a second-half substitute. Although he didn't score, his impact was immediate, as he linked up well with his teammates and created several chances. The experience of playing at Wembley, under the lights, with the entire nation watching, was something Cole would never forget.

Euro 2024: Making His Mark on the Biggest Stage

Just months after his senior debut, Cole was selected as part of the England squad for Euro 2024. The tournament, held in Germany, was a major milestone in Cole's career, as it offered him the chance to showcase his talent on one of the biggest stages in international football.

England entered the tournament with high hopes, and Cole was determined to make his mark. He featured prominently throughout the group stages, playing in matches against Italy, Ukraine, and Austria. His performances were characterized by his usual blend of creativity, vision, and technical skill. In the match against Ukraine, Cole provided a crucial assist, threading a perfectly weighted pass through the defense for Harry Kane to score.

As England progressed to the knockout stages, the pressure intensified. The quarter-final against Spain was one of the most challenging matches of the tournament. The game was a tactical battle, with both teams struggling to break each other down. In the 68th minute, with the score tied at 1-1, Cole was brought on to add some attacking impetus.

His impact was immediate. Within minutes, he found himself in possession on the edge of the box, surrounded by Spanish defenders. With a quick turn and a deft touch, he created space for himself and unleashed a shot that was tipped over the bar by the Spanish goalkeeper. While the match eventually went to penalties, where England emerged victorious, Cole's contribution had been vital in pushing the team forward.

In the semi-final, England faced Germany in what was a repeat of the Under-21 final just a year earlier. The atmosphere was electric, and the stakes couldn't have been higher. Cole played with composure and maturity beyond his years, helping England control the midfield and create chances. Although England lost narrowly, Cole's performances throughout the tournament had solidified his place in the squad.

The Influence of International Football

Playing for England at the senior level was more than just an honor for Cole—it was a transformative experience that shaped him as a player. The intensity of international football, the pressure of representing his country, and the experience of competing against the best in the world pushed Cole to new heights.

"The thing about playing for England is that you're always up against the best," Cole said in an interview after the tournament. "Every match is a test, and it forces you to raise your game. It's made me a better player, without a doubt."

The camaraderie within the England squad was also something that Cole cherished. Training and playing alongside players from different clubs, each bringing their own style and experience, was an opportunity to learn and grow. The bond he formed with his teammates, united by the goal of bringing glory to their country, was something he would carry with him throughout his career.

As Cole looked ahead to the future, he knew that his journey with England was just beginning. The experiences he had gained at Euro 2024, the lessons learned, and the memories made would stay with him forever. And as he continued to dream big, Cole was determined to keep giving his all for the Three Lions, proud to wear the shirt and represent his country on the world stage.

CHAPTER 8: A NEW CHAPTER AT CHELSEA

The summer of 2023 was a whirlwind for Cole Palmer. Fresh off a historic treble-winning season with Manchester City, Cole found himself at a crossroads in his career. While he had grown immensely under Pep Guardiola's guidance, the time had come for a new challenge—one that would allow him to step out of the shadows and carve out his own legacy. That challenge presented itself in the form of a transfer to Chelsea.

The Transfer: A Bold Move

The decision to leave Manchester City was not an easy one for Cole. City had been his home since he was a young boy, and the club had played a crucial role in his development. But as the 2023 summer transfer window opened, it became clear that Chelsea was keen on bringing him to Stamford Bridge. The London club was in the midst of a rebuild under their new manager, Mauricio Pochettino, and they saw Cole as a key part of their future.

The negotiations between the clubs were intense, with Chelsea eventually agreeing to a deal worth an initial £40 million, with potential add-ons increasing the fee to £42.5 million. For Cole, the move represented a significant step forward in his career. He would now have the opportunity to play more regularly and take on a more prominent role in the team.

Behind the scenes, the decision was influenced by several factors. Guardiola, while keen to keep Cole, understood the young midfielder's desire for more playing time. "I've learned so much from Pep, and I'll always be grateful for that," Cole said in an interview after the transfer was finalized. "But I'm at a point in my career where I need to be playing regularly, and Chelsea is offering me that opportunity."

Mauricio Pochettino was also instrumental in persuading Cole to make the move. The Argentine manager had a reputation for developing young talent, and his vision for Chelsea's future aligned perfectly with Cole's ambitions. "Cole is a player with immense potential," Pochettino said during his first press conference after the transfer. "He's young, hungry, and has the qualities we need to take this team forward."

The Debut: Making an Impact

Cole didn't have to wait long to make his debut for Chelsea. Just days after completing his transfer, he was named in the squad for Chelsea's Premier League match against Nottingham Forest. As he walked out onto the pitch at Stamford Bridge, wearing the blue of Chelsea for the first time, Cole felt a surge of excitement. This was the start of a new chapter in his career, and he was determined to make an impact.

The match itself was a closely contested affair, with Forest defending resolutely. Cole was brought on as a second-half substitute, and while he couldn't find the back of the net, his quick feet and sharp passing immediately caught the eye of the Chelsea faithful. The match ended in a narrow 1-0 defeat for Chelsea, but for Cole, it was the beginning of what would be an exciting journey.

Just a few weeks later, Cole scored his first goal for Chelsea in a match against Burnley. It was a typical rainy day in the north of England, and the conditions were tough, but Cole thrived. In the 60th minute, Chelsea was awarded a penalty after a clumsy challenge by a Burnley defender. As the players debated who should take it, Pochettino signaled for Cole to step up. The young midfielder placed the ball on the spot, took a deep breath, and coolly slotted it into the bottom corner, sending the goalkeeper the wrong way.

The goal was celebrated wildly by both Cole and his teammates. As he ran towards the corner flag, he was quickly surrounded by his fellow players, who congratulated him on his first Chelsea goal. "That was a big moment for me," Cole said after the match. "Scoring my first goal for Chelsea, in front of our fans, was something I'll never forget."

Key Performances: Rising to the Occasion

Cole's early performances for Chelsea quickly endeared him to the fans. His creativity, work rate, and ability to make things happen on the pitch made him a key player in Pochettino's system. One of his standout performances came in a thrilling London derby against Tottenham Hotspur.

The match was played at a frantic pace, with both teams creating numerous chances. Cole was instrumental in Chelsea's attack, linking up well with the likes of Raheem Sterling and Nicolas Jackson. In the 75th minute, with the score tied at 1-1, Cole picked up the ball on the edge of the box, dribbled past two Tottenham defenders, and fired a low shot into the bottom corner. The goal proved to be the match-winner, and Chelsea secured a crucial 2-1 victory.

Pochettino was full of praise for Cole after the match. "Cole was outstanding today," he said. "He's shown that he can perform at the highest level, and his goal was the difference. We're very fortunate to have him here at Chelsea."

Another memorable moment came in a high-stakes match against Manchester City, his former club. The build-up to the game was filled with anticipation, as it was the first time Cole would face City since leaving the club. The match lived up to the hype, with both teams playing attacking football.

In the dying moments of the game, with the score locked at 3-3, Chelsea was awarded a penalty after a handball by a City defender. There was no doubt about who would take it—Cole stepped up, his face a picture of concentration. He sent the City goalkeeper the wrong way, calmly slotting the ball into the net to give Chelsea a dramatic 4-3 victory.

After the match, Cole was approached by several of his former City teammates. "You played well, mate," Kevin De Bruyne said, patting him on the back. "But you couldn't let us have that one, could you?"

Cole smiled, knowing that this was just part of

the game. "It felt a bit strange playing against City," he admitted in a post-match interview. "But I'm a Chelsea player now, and I'm here to give my all for this club."

Building a Legacy at Chelsea

As the season progressed, Cole's influence at Chelsea continued to grow. He became a regular starter, and his performances were crucial in helping Chelsea climb the Premier League table. His versatility allowed Pochettino to deploy him in various roles, whether as a winger, a central midfielder, or even as a false nine.

Cole's impact on the team was not just limited to his performances on the pitch. His positive attitude, work ethic, and willingness to learn quickly made him a favorite in the dressing room. "Cole's been fantastic since he joined," said Chelsea captain Thiago Silva. "He's young, but he's got a mature head on his shoulders. He's always willing to put in the extra work, and that's the kind of mentality we need here."

Pochettino also spoke highly of Cole's contributions. "Cole has adapted very quickly to life at Chelsea," the manager said in a press conference. "He's a very intelligent player, and he's shown that he can handle the pressure of playing for a big club. We're very excited about what he can achieve here."

Looking ahead, Cole knew that there was still much more to accomplish. He was determined to help Chelsea win trophies and to continue developing as a player. "I've always dreamed big," Cole said in an interview. "I want to win everything I can with Chelsea, and I want to keep improving every day. I'm in the right place to do that."

As Cole settled into life at Chelsea, he reflected on how far he had come—from the streets of Wythenshawe to playing for one of the biggest clubs in the world. The journey had been incredible, and he knew that the best was yet to come. With the support of his new teammates and the belief of his manager, Cole Palmer was ready to write the next chapter of his footballing story—a chapter filled with ambition, determination, and the pursuit   of   greatness.

CHAPTER 9: NAVIGATING NEW CHALLENGES

Stepping into the spotlight at Chelsea brought with it a new set of challenges for Cole Palmer. The expectations were higher, the competition was fierce, and the pressure to justify his hefty transfer fee weighed heavily on his shoulders. But as Cole had done throughout his career, he faced these challenges head-on, determined to prove himself and establish his place among the elite.

The Pressure of Expectations

From the moment Cole arrived at Chelsea, the spotlight was on him. The £40 million transfer fee was a significant investment, and both the fans and the media were eager to see if the young midfielder could live up to the price tag. There were whispers of doubt, comparisons to other young talents who had struggled to adapt, and questions about whether he could handle the pressure of playing for one of the biggest clubs in the world.

Cole was well aware of the scrutiny. "I knew coming to Chelsea was a big step," he admitted in an early-season interview. "There's always going to be pressure when you move for a big fee, but I've always believed in myself. I know what I can bring to the team, and I'm here to work hard and show that I belong."

The transition to life in London was also a significant change for Cole. Having spent most of his life in Manchester, moving to a new city, away from his family and familiar surroundings, was challenging. The demands of adapting to a new team, a new tactical system under Mauricio Pochettino, and the high expectations of the Chelsea fans added to the pressure.

But Cole was determined to make the most of this opportunity. He knew that to succeed, he would have to embrace these challenges, stay focused, and continue working hard in training. "It's about taking things one step at a time," he told his teammates. "I just need to keep doing what I do best, and the rest will follow."

Adapting to Life at Chelsea

One of the biggest challenges Cole faced was adapting to the tactical demands of Pochettino's system. The Argentine manager was known for his high-intensity, pressing style of play, which required players to be both physically and mentally sharp. Cole quickly realized that he would need to raise his game to meet these demands.

In training, Pochettino was constantly pushing Cole to improve. "You've got the talent, Cole," Pochettino would often say during their sessions. "But talent isn't enough at this level. You need to be quicker, stronger, and more decisive. Keep working, and you'll get there."

Cole took these words to heart. He dedicated himself to improving his fitness, spending extra hours in the gym to build his strength and endurance. He also focused on his tactical understanding, studying video footage of Chelsea's matches to better understand Pochettino's system and his role within it.

The hard work began to pay off. Cole's performances on the pitch improved with each game, as he started to find his rhythm in the team. His versatility allowed him to play in various positions, whether on the wing, in central midfield, or even as a forward, and his ability to adapt quickly earned him praise from both his teammates and his manager.

"Cole's been brilliant," said Reece James,

Chelsea's captain, in an interview. "He's come in, put his head down, and worked hard every day. You can see the quality he has, and he's been a big part of our team this season."

Overcoming Doubts and Proving Himself

Despite the positive signs, there were still moments of doubt. In the early months of the season, there were games where Cole struggled to make an impact, where the pressure seemed to get to him. The media was quick to jump on these performances, questioning whether Chelsea had overpaid for the young midfielder.

But Cole remained resilient. He knew that setbacks were a part of football and that the only way to overcome them was to keep pushing forward. He leaned on the support of his family, his teammates, and the coaching staff, all of whom believed in his potential.

One particularly challenging period came in November, when Chelsea faced a string of tough fixtures against top Premier League teams. In a match against Liverpool at Anfield, Cole started but struggled to influence the game. Chelsea lost 2-1, and Cole was substituted in the second half. The criticism that followed was harsh, with some questioning whether he was ready for the Premier

League's biggest challenges.

But rather than letting the criticism affect him, Cole used it as motivation. "I knew I had to do better," he reflected later. "It wasn't my best performance, but I've always believed that you learn more from the tough times than the good ones. I just needed to keep my head down and keep working."

The turning point came a few weeks later in a match against West Ham United. Chelsea had been struggling to find consistency, and the pressure was mounting. Pochettino decided to start Cole in a more central role, giving him the responsibility of orchestrating the team's attacks.

From the first whistle, Cole played with a determination and confidence that had been building over the past few months. He was everywhere on the pitch, driving forward with the ball, creating chances, and linking up play. In the 65th minute, with the score tied at 1-1, Cole received the ball just outside the penalty area, took a quick touch to his left, and curled a beautiful shot into the top corner.

The goal was a statement—a reminder of the talent that had brought him to Chelsea in the first place. The fans erupted in celebration, and as Cole was mobbed by his teammates, the weight of the previous weeks seemed to lift from his shoulders.

After the match, Pochettino was full of praise. "That was the Cole we know," he said in his post-match interview. "He's been working so hard, and today he showed why we brought him here. He's got a big future at this club."

Managing the Demands of Elite Football

As the season progressed, Cole continued to grow into his role at Chelsea. But with the increased responsibilities came the challenges of managing the physical and mental demands of playing at the highest level.

Cole had always been a hard worker, but the intensity of Premier League football, combined with the expectations that came with his transfer, required him to find new ways to stay at his best. Recovery became a key focus, with Cole working closely with the club's medical and fitness staff to ensure he could perform consistently.

"It's not just about what you do on the pitch," Cole explained in an interview. "Recovery, nutrition, mental preparation—it all plays a part. I've learned that to play at this level, you need to take care of every aspect of your game."

COLE: THE NEXT BIG THING

One of the ways Cole managed the mental demands was by maintaining a strong support network. He regularly spoke with his family, who kept him grounded and reminded him of how far he had come. He also found a mentor in Thiago Silva, who, with his vast experience, offered invaluable advice on how to handle the pressures of top-level football.

"Thiago's been amazing," Cole said. "He's been through it all, and he's always there with a word of advice or encouragement. Having someone like that in the dressing room makes a big difference."

Establishing Himself as a Key Player

By the time the season reached its midway point, Cole had firmly established himself as a key player for Chelsea. His performances were consistent, and he had become a regular starter in Pochettino's team. The fans, who had initially been unsure about his signing, were now fully behind him, chanting his name from the stands.

Cole's ability to rise to the occasion in big matches continued to impress. In a crucial Champions League group stage match against AC Milan, Cole played a starring role, scoring one goal and assisting another in a 3-1 victory that secured

Chelsea's place in the knockout stages.

Reflecting on his journey, Cole knew that there were still challenges ahead, but he also knew that he had the tools to overcome them. "This season has been a learning experience," he said. "I've had ups and downs, but I've come through it stronger. I'm excited about what the future holds, and I'm ready to keep pushing myself to new levels."

As Cole looked forward to the rest of the season, he was filled with a renewed sense of purpose. The challenges he had faced had only made him more determined, and he was ready to continue proving himself, not just as a player who could justify his transfer fee, but as a player who could make a lasting impact at Chelsea.

CHAPTER 10: VERSATILITY AND GROWTH UNDER TOP MANAGERS

Cole Palmer's journey in football has been shaped by his experiences under two of the most respected managers in the game: Pep Guardiola at Manchester City and Mauricio Pochettino at Chelsea. Each manager brought a unique approach to the game, and Cole's development under their guidance has been a testament to his adaptability, intelligence, and versatility on the field.

Learning Under Guardiola: The Pep Effect

Pep Guardiola is known for his tactical genius, his ability to develop young talent, and his demanding approach to football. At Manchester City, Guardiola's influence on Cole Palmer was profound. Guardiola's philosophy is centered around positional play, where every player is expected to understand and execute their role with precision. For Cole, this meant learning to be not just a skilled player, but a tactically astute one as well.

From the moment Cole broke into the first team at City, Guardiola pushed him to develop his understanding of the game. Training sessions were intense, with Guardiola often stopping play to explain the finer details of positioning, movement, and decision-making. "Pep is all about the details," Cole once remarked. "He's always looking for ways to improve your game, and he doesn't let anything slip by. You have to be switched on all the time."

One of the key aspects of Cole's development under Guardiola was his versatility. At City, Cole was often deployed in different positions— sometimes on the wing, sometimes in central midfield, and occasionally even as a false nine. Guardiola believed that a player's understanding of multiple roles would make them more effective and adaptable on the pitch. Cole embraced this philosophy, learning to play with intelligence and fluidity, regardless of where he was positioned.

A memorable example of Cole's versatility came during a Champions League match against Paris Saint-Germain in the 2021-2022 season. With City needing a win to secure top spot in their group, Guardiola deployed Cole on the right wing. Throughout the match, Cole was tasked with both attacking responsibilities and defensive duties, tracking back to help the team while also providing width in the attack. His ability to adapt to the demands of the game was crucial in City's 2-1 victory.

Guardiola's influence extended beyond tactics. He was also instrumental in helping Cole develop the mental aspects of his game. The pressure of playing for a club like Manchester City, with expectations of winning every match and competing for every trophy, could be overwhelming. Guardiola helped Cole learn how to cope with this pressure, instilling a mindset of continuous improvement and resilience. "At City, you're expected to win every game, every trophy," Cole said. "Pep taught me how to handle that pressure and keep pushing myself to get better."

Growing Under Pochettino: A New Chapter

When Cole moved to Chelsea in 2023, he found himself under the guidance of Mauricio Pochettino, a manager known for his ability to nurture young talent and build cohesive teams. Pochettino's approach was different from Guardiola's, but it was equally influential in Cole's development.

Pochettino emphasized the importance of physicality, high-intensity pressing, and teamwork. Under his guidance, Cole continued to develop his versatility, but he also became a more complete player in terms of physical and mental endurance. Pochettino's training sessions were grueling, with a focus on fitness and tactical discipline. Cole quickly adapted to this new environment, understanding that to succeed at Chelsea, he needed to bring a different level of energy and commitment.

One of the key differences between Guardiola and Pochettino was their approach to man-management. While Guardiola was more intense and focused on tactical details, Pochettino took a more holistic approach, emphasizing the importance of building strong relationships with his players. Pochettino was known for his ability to create a close-knit squad, and he made a point of getting to know Cole personally, understanding what motivated him both on and off the pitch.

"Poch is like a mentor," Cole explained. "He's always there to talk to you, to offer advice, not just about football but about life. He's helped me settle in at Chelsea and made sure I feel confident in my role in the team."

This personal touch from Pochettino was evident in how Cole performed on the pitch. One of the standout moments of the 2023-2024 season came in a Premier League match against Tottenham

Hotspur. Pochettino, understanding Cole's strengths, deployed him in a more central attacking role, allowing him to dictate the tempo of the game. Cole responded with a masterful performance, scoring a goal and providing an assist in a 3-1 victory. It was a clear demonstration of how Pochettino's trust in Cole had allowed him to flourish.

Versatility: The Key to Success

One of the defining characteristics of Cole Palmer's career has been his versatility. Whether playing under Guardiola at City or Pochettino at Chelsea, Cole's ability to adapt to different roles and tactical demands has made him an indispensable player for both club and country.

At Manchester City, Cole's versatility was evident in his ability to play across multiple positions. Guardiola often used him as a winger, where his pace and dribbling ability allowed him to stretch defenses, but he also trusted Cole to play in central midfield, where his vision and passing could unlock opposition defenses. This flexibility made Cole a valuable asset in Guardiola's rotational system, where players were expected to fill different roles depending on the needs of the team.

At Chelsea, Cole's versatility has continued to be

a key asset. Pochettino has used him in various positions, from an attacking midfielder to a wide forward. This ability to adapt has made Cole a crucial part of Chelsea's tactical setup, especially in big games where flexibility and unpredictability are often the difference between winning and losing.

One particular match that highlighted Cole's versatility was a Champions League clash against Real Madrid in the knockout stages. With Chelsea facing a tough task against the defending champions, Pochettino deployed Cole in a deeper midfield role, where he was responsible for breaking up play and initiating counter-attacks. Despite being in an unfamiliar position, Cole excelled, helping Chelsea secure a 2-1 victory that sent them through to the next round.

Cole's versatility has also made him indispensable for the England national team. Whether playing for the Under-21s or the senior team, Cole has been used in a variety of roles, always adapting to the needs of the team. His ability to play in different positions has given England's managers tactical flexibility, allowing them to switch formations and strategies without losing effectiveness.

Looking Ahead: A Player for All Seasons

As Cole continues to develop under Pochettino at Chelsea, his versatility and growth as a player have set him up for a bright future. Whether playing as a winger, a central midfielder, or even as a forward, Cole has shown that he can excel in any role, making him a valuable asset for both club and country.

Reflecting on his journey so far, Cole is grateful for the opportunities he's had to learn from two of the best managers in the game. "Playing under Pep and Poch has been an incredible experience," he said. "They've both taught me so much, in different ways. I've learned to be versatile, to adapt, and to always be ready for whatever challenge comes my way."

As he looks ahead to the future, Cole is focused on continuing to grow as a player, to keep learning and improving. "I know there's still a lot I can achieve," he said. "I want to keep pushing myself, to keep making an impact, and to help my teams win as much as possible. I'm excited about what's to come."

With his versatility, work ethic, and the lessons he's learned from two top managers, Cole Palmer is well on his way to becoming one of the best players of his generation. Whether at Chelsea, for England, or wherever his career takes him, Cole is ready to continue his journey, always striving for greatness.

CHAPTER 11: SHAPING THE FUTURE AT CHELSEA

With every game, every training session, and every moment on the pitch, Cole Palmer was carving out a legacy at Chelsea. The journey that had begun in the streets of Wythenshawe and blossomed under the guidance of Guardiola and Pochettino was now reaching new heights. But with that growth came new responsibilities, and Cole was increasingly aware of the role he needed to play—not just as a player, but as a leader in a team looking to return to the pinnacle of English and European football.

Emerging as a Leader

As the 2023-2024 season wore on, it became clear that Cole Palmer was more than just another talented player in Chelsea's ranks. His performances on the pitch were consistently strong, but it was his attitude off the pitch that truly set him apart. Cole had always been known for his work ethic and humility, and now, as he matured, those qualities began to manifest in leadership.

During one of Chelsea's training sessions, Pochettino noticed Cole staying behind after the session had ended, working on his passing and shooting. This wasn't new—Cole often put in extra hours—but what caught Pochettino's eye was the group of younger players who had gathered around Cole, watching and learning.

Pochettino walked over and patted Cole on the back. "You're setting a great example, Cole," he said. "Keep this up, and you'll be leading this team in no time."

Cole smiled, grateful for the recognition, but for him, this was just part of the job. "I've always believed that hard work is contagious," he explained in an interview later that week. "If I can inspire the younger guys to put in the extra work, then we'll all get better together."

His leadership on the pitch was just as evident. In a crucial Champions League knockout match against Juventus, Chelsea was trailing 1-0 in the second half. The team was struggling to break down Juventus' defense, and the tension was palpable. Sensing the need for a change in approach, Cole took it upon himself to rally the team.

"Let's keep pushing! We're still in this!" he shouted to his teammates as he urged them forward. His energy and determination were infectious, and it wasn't long before Chelsea found the equalizer, with Cole himself providing the assist for the goal. The match ended in a 2-1 victory for Chelsea, and as the final whistle blew, it was clear that Cole's leadership had been a driving force behind the comeback.

Building Chemistry with Teammates

A key aspect of Cole's success at Chelsea was the chemistry he built with his teammates. Football is a team sport, and no player, no matter how talented, can succeed alone. Cole understood this better than most, and he worked hard to develop strong connections with those around him.

His relationship with Chelsea's star winger Raheem Sterling was particularly important. The two had played together briefly at Manchester City, but it was at Chelsea where their partnership truly flourished. On the pitch, they seemed to have an almost telepathic understanding, with Cole's quick passes and Sterling's blistering pace causing problems for defenses across the Premier League.

"Playing with Raheem is amazing," Cole said.

"He's so fast and sharp. I know that if I can get the ball to him in the right spot, he'll do the rest. We push each other to be better, and that's what makes our partnership so strong."

But it wasn't just Sterling. Cole made it a point to build relationships with all his teammates, from veteran players like Thiago Silva to the younger members of the squad. He believed that a strong, unified team was the key to success, and he did everything he could to foster that unity.

In a team meeting after a tough loss to Manchester United, Cole was one of the first to speak up. "We're better than this," he said, his voice steady but firm. "We need to stick together, keep working, and trust in what we're building here. We've got the talent—we just need to show it."

His words resonated with the team, and in the matches that followed, Chelsea's performances improved. The players fought harder, played with more cohesion, and began to climb the Premier League table.

Eyeing Future Success

As the season neared its end, Cole's focus remained on the future. Chelsea was in the hunt for a top-four finish in the Premier League, and there was still the possibility of lifting silverware in the FA Cup or the Champions League. But for Cole, it wasn't just about the immediate goals—it was about building something lasting.

"I want to help Chelsea get back to where we belong—at the top of English and European football," he said in an interview. "But it's not just about this season. It's about laying the foundation for sustained success. We've got a great squad, a great manager, and a great club. Now it's about putting all the pieces together."

Pochettino shared Cole's vision for the future. The manager saw in Cole a player who could be a cornerstone for Chelsea for years to come. "Cole has the potential to be one of the best," Pochettino said. "He's got the talent, the work ethic, and the leadership qualities you need to succeed at this level. I'm excited to see where he can take us."

As the season drew to a close, Cole's thoughts turned to the future. He knew there were still many challenges ahead, but he was ready for them. Whether it was leading Chelsea to victory in a cup final, securing a top-four finish, or helping the team succeed in Europe, Cole was determined to give his all.

He also kept an eye on his long-term goals. Cole knew that to achieve everything he wanted in his career, he would need to continue improving, continue leading, and continue dreaming big. He was ready to take on whatever came next, confident in the path he was on and excited for the journey ahead.

With his eyes firmly set on the future, Cole Palmer was not just shaping his own destiny—he was helping to shape the future of Chelsea Football Club.

CHAPTER 12: TRIVIA

Theme: Chelsea Football Club

Questions:
1. In which year was Chelsea FC founded?
2. Who is the all-time top scorer for Chelsea?
3. How many times has Chelsea won the Premier League?
4. What is the name of Chelsea's home stadium?
5. Who was Chelsea's manager when they won their first UEFA Champions League?
6. In what year did Chelsea win their first FA Cup?
7. From which club did Chelsea sign Eden Hazard?
8. Who was the first Chelsea player to win the Ballon d'Or?
9. In which season did Chelsea achieve their highest points total in the Premier League?
10. What are Chelsea FC's official club colors?

Answers:

1. 1905.
2.   Frank Lampard.
3.   5 times (as of 2023).
4.   Stamford Bridge.
5.   Roberto Di Matteo.
6.   1970.
7.   Lille OSC.
8.   No Chelsea player has won the Ballon d'Or as of 2023.
9.   2004-05 season (95 points).
10.   Royal blue and white.

Theme: English Football

Questions:
1.   When was the Football Association (FA) formed in England?
2.   Which team won the first ever Football League in England?
3.   Who is the all-time top scorer of the England national football team?
4.   In what year was the Premier League founded?
5.   How manyteams   compete   in   the   English   Football   League Championship?
6.   What is the oldest professional football club in England?
7.   Who was the first English football club to win a European Cup?
8.   What is the maximum number of substitutes a team can make in an official English league match?
9.   Which English club has the most FA Cup wins?
10.   Who holds the record for the most Premier League appearances?

Answers:

1. 1863.
2.   Preston North End.
3.   Wayne Rooney.
4.   1992.
5.   24.
6.   Notts County.
7.   Manchester United.
8.   3 (excluding concussion substitutes).
9.   Arsenal.
10.   Gareth Barry.

Theme: Young Football Talents

Questions:

1. Who won the Golden Boy award in 2021?
2. At what age did Lionel Messi make his professional debut?
3. Who is the youngest player to ever play in the World Cup?
4. Which young player was named Best Young Player in the 2018 FIFA World Cup?
5. At what age did Cristiano Ronaldo sign with Manchester United?
6. Who is the youngest player to score in a UEFA Champions League final?
7. Which player was the youngest to reach 100 appearances in the Premier League?
8. Who is the youngest captain to win a UEFA Champions League?
9. At what age did Wayne Rooney make his professional debut?
10. Who was the first teenager to score in two consecutive World Cup tournaments?

Answers:
1. Pedri.
2. 17.
3. Norman Whiteside.
4. Kylian Mbappé.
5. 18.
6. Patrick Kluivert.
7. Michael Owen.
8. Iker Casillas.
9. 16.
10. Pelé.

Theme: Premier League

Questions:

1. Which team won the inaugural Premier League season?

2. Who holds the record for the most Premier League goals scored?

3. Which team holds the record for the highest points total in a single Premier League season?

4. Who was the first player to reach 100 assists in the Premier League?

5. What is the highest number of goals scored by a team in a single Premier League match?

6. Who is the youngest manager to win a Premier League title?

7. What is the record for the longest unbeaten run in the Premier League?

8. Who was the first non-European player to win the Premier League Golden Boot?

9. Which club was the first to be relegated from the Premier League?

10. Who is the oldest player to have played in the Premier League?

Answers:

1.   Manchester United.
2.   Alan Shearer.
3.   Manchester City (100 points, 2017-2018 season).
4.   Ryan Giggs.
5.   9 goals.
6.   José Mourinho.
7.   49 games (Arsenal).
8.   Didier Drogba.
9.   Crystal Palace.
10.   John Burridge.

COLE: THE NEXT BIG THING

Theme: Football in the 2020s

Questions:
1.   Who won the 2020 UEFA European Championship?
2.   Which club won the 2020-2021 UEFA Champions League?
3.   Who was the FIFA Best Men's Player in 2020?
4.   In which city was the 2022 FIFA World Cup held?
5.   Who is the most expensive football transfer as of 2023?
6.   What new rule regarding substitutes was introduced in football post- 2020?
7.   Which team won the Copa America in 2021?
8.   Who was the top scorer in the 2020-2021 English Premier League season?
9.   Which national team won the inaugural UEFA Nations League in 2019?
10.   What significant change occurred in the offside rule in the 2020s?

Answers:
1.　Italy.
2.　Chelsea.
3.　Robert Lewandowski.
4.　Doha, Qatar.
5.　Neymar Jr. (to Paris Saint-Germain).
6.　The introduction of five substitutes in a match.
7.　Argentina.
8.　Harry Kane.
9.　Portugal.
10.　The use of VAR (Video Assistant Referee) to determine offside decisions.

CHAPTER 13: FUN FOOTBALL FACTS

Historical Milestones

- The first live broadcast of a football match was in 1937: a match between Arsenal's first and reserve teams.
- Sheffield FC, founded in 1857, is recognized as the world's oldest existing football club.
- The first ever international football match was between Scotland and England in 1872.

Remarkable Matches

- The 1964 "Fog Match": A European Cup match between Liverpool and Ajax was played in such dense fog, fans couldn't see the game.
- The 2002 World Cup featured a match between South Korea and Italy, where South Korea advanced, marking a significant underdog victory.

Innovative Tactics and Strategies

- The 'WM' formation, developed in the 1920s by Herbert Chapman of Arsenal, revolutionized football tactics.
- Netherlands' "Total Football" strategy in the

1970s changed the way the game was played, focusing on player versatility.

Player Achievements and Records

- Norman Whiteside is the youngest player to ever play in a World Cup, at the age of 17 years and 41 days in 1982.
- Roger Milla of Cameroon became the oldest goal scorer in a World Cup at age 42 in 1994.

Cultural Impact

- In the 1998 World Cup, Jamaica's team, known as the 'Reggae Boyz', brought widespread attention to Caribbean football.
- Iceland's national team features more filmmakers than professional players, a unique aspect of their 2018 World Cup squad.

Technological Advancements

- Goal-line technology was first used in a FIFA World Cup in 2014 to eliminate goal-scoring controversies.
- The first football video game, "NASL Soccer," was released in 1980 for the

Intellivision console.

Women's Football

- Lily Parr, a star of the women's team Dick, Kerr Ladies, scored over 900 goals in her career from 1919 to 1951.
- The first women's football match to draw a sizable crowd was in 1920, with 53,000 spectators at Goodison Park.

Unique Matches and Tournaments

- The 'Christmas Truce' match in 1914 during World War I, where soldiers from opposing sides played football on the battlefield.
- The first indoor professional league, the Major Indoor Soccer League (MISL), was founded in the USA in 1978.

Famous Football Clubs

- Real Madrid was named 'Club of the Century' by FIFA in 2000, celebrating its rich history and achievements.
- Celtic FC in Scotland was the first British team to win the European Cup in 1967.

Football in Literature and Media

- The first football film, "The Great Game," was released in 1930, focusing on the drama of football in England.
- The book "Fever Pitch" by Nick Hornby, published in 1992, is one of the most famous football-themed books, detailing a fan's love for Arsenal FC.

Football and Society

- During the 1969 'Football War', El Salvador and Honduras went to war partly due to tensions after a football match.
- The 'Match of Peace' in 2014, initiated by Pope Francis, brought together world football stars to promote peace and unity.

Remarkable Coaches and Management

- Vicente del Bosque is the only football manager to have won the Champions League, European Championship, and World Cup.
- Helenio Herrera, an Argentine coach, popularized the defensive strategy of 'Catenaccio' in Italian football during the 1960s.

Football and Politics

- The 1973 Chile vs USSR World Cup qualifier was forfeited by the USSR due to political reasons, sending Chile to the World Cup.
- The 'Celtic Tiger' economic boom in Ireland in the 1990s is partly attributed to the national team's success in the 1990 World Cup.

Unusual Football Rules and Occurrences

- In 1998, a match in Congo was struck by lightning, affecting all 22 players and leading to bizarre and tragic consequences.
- The 'Golden Goal' rule, used in the 1990s and early 2000s, allowed the first team to score in extra time to win the match immediately.

Football Superstitions and Rituals

- Many players, like Pelé and Johan Cruyff, had specific pre-match rituals or superstitions they believed brought good luck.
- Brazilian club Vasco da Gama once hired an exorcist to break their losing streak in the late 20th century.

Stadiums and Architecture

- The Maracanã Stadium in Brazil was once the largest in the world, with a capacity of nearly 200,000 in the 1950s.
- FC Barcelona's Camp Nou is the largest stadium in Europe, with a capacity of over 99,000 spectators.

Football in Art and Music

- The song "Three Lions," released during Euro '96, became an iconic football anthem in England.
- Banksy, the anonymous street artist, has created several football- themed artworks, reflecting the sport's influence on culture.

Influential Football Events

- The Bosman ruling in 1995 changed football transfers forever, allowing players more freedom to move after their contracts ended.
- The Heysel Stadium disaster in 1985 led to English clubs being banned from European competitions for five years.

Youth Football and Academies

- Barcelona's La Masia is one of the most famous youth academies, producing players like Lionel Messi and Xavi Hernandez.
- Ajax Amsterdam's youth academy is known for its emphasis on technical skills, producing talents like Johan Cruyff and Dennis Bergkamp.

Global Reach of Football

- Greenland has one of the world's most challenging football environments due to its harsh climate and lack of grass fields.
- Bhutan and Montserrat, two of the world's lowest-ranked teams, played a match in 2002 dubbed "The Other Final," coinciding with the World Cup final.

Football and Health

- Studies show that playing football regularly can significantly improve cardiovascular health and overall fitness.
- Professional footballers run an average of 10 to 12 kilometers per match, showcasing the sport's physical demands.

Football and Education

- Many clubs like Ajax and Manchester United, have education programs for their youth players to ensure academic development.
- Football has been used as a tool for social development and education in countries like Brazil and South Africa.

Football and Fashion

- The trend of footballers becoming fashion icons began in the 1960s, with players like George Best leading the way.
- Football kits have evolved significantly over the years, reflecting changes in fashion and technology.

Innovations in Football Training

- The use of GPS tracking vests in training has revolutionized how coaches understand players' physical performance.
- Virtual reality technology is increasingly being used for tactical training and simulating match situations.

FOOTY JOKE CORNER

- What did the referee say to the chicken who tripped an opponent? "That's a fowl!"
- What's black and white, then black and white, then black and white again? A Newcastle supporter tumbling down a slope!
- I left two Everton tickets on my car dashboard yesterday. When I returned, someone had broken the window and left two more.
- Why was the football player sad on his birthday? He received a red card!
- What do you call someone who stands between goalposts and stops the ball from escaping? Annette!
- England's playing Iceland tomorrow. If they win, they're up against Tesco next week, followed by Asda.
- Which football team is a fan of desserts? Aston Vanilla!
- Where's the best place in the U.S. to buy a football uniform? New Jersey!
- What do Lionel Messi and a magician share in common? They both can pull off hat-tricks!
- The new coach of our struggling football team is strict. Last weekend, he caught two fans trying to leave early. He told them, "Get back

in there and watch till the end!"

- Why did Cinderella get removed from the football team? She kept avoiding the ball!
- What's a goalie's favorite meal? Beans on the post!
- Why don't grasshoppers watch football? They're cricket fans!
- What's a ghost's preferred football position? Ghoulkeeper!
- Why did the coach bring pencils to the locker room before the match?
- He was hoping for a draw!
- Did you hear about the new Everton Bra? Great support, but no cups! Who was the top scorer in the Greek Mythology League? The centaur striker!
- What did the coach do when the field was flooded? He sent in the subs!
- My partner broke up with me because of my football obsession. I'm a bit down – we'd been together for three seasons.
- What ship can hold 20 football teams but only three leave each season? The Premier-ship!
- What's the difference between Bournemouth and a tea bag? The tea bag remains in the cup

longer!

- Why was the world's best football player told to clean their room?
- Because it was Messi!
- Which part of the football field smells the best? The scent-er spot!
- Why did the football ball quit? It was tired of being kicked around! What do you call a Brentford fan after their team wins the Premier League? Dreaming!
- Why aren't football stadiums in space? Lack of atmosphere!
- Why do football players remind you of toddlers? Both love to dribble! God and Satan decided to settle their differences with a football match. God said, "All the good players come to heaven." Satan smirked, "But we have all the referees."
- Which football team has their tactics down? The Hammers.
- Why did the football player hold his shoe to his ear? He loved sole tunes!
- What's the coldest stadium in the Premiership? Icy Trafford!
- Which team begins every match with energy?

The Gunners!

- What runs around the football field but never moves? The sideline!
- Which team is the stickiest? The Toffees!
- Best position if you don't like football? Right back – in the locker room!
- My computer caught the 'Bad-Goalie Virus'. It can't save a thing.
- Why did the football field turn into a triangle? Someone took its corner! Why did the football captain bring a rope to the field? He was the skipper!
- How do football players keep cool? They stay close to the fans!
- What do you call a Norwich player in the World Cup's knockout stages? The ref!

GUESS WHO

Riddle 1:

In Manchester's blue, I stand tall and proud, A Belgian master, in skill unbound.
With passes that weave like a beautiful art, In the City's midfield, I play my part.
Who am I, with vision so smart?

Riddle 2:

From Ukraine's fields to the English stage, In

blue I sprint, with youthful rage.

A winger fast, with skillful feet, At Chelsea's side, I'm hard to beat. Who am I, with pace so fleet?

Riddle 3:

In England's squad, I'm a star so bright, At City's heart, I play with might.

In defence or midfield, I've made my name, With tenacity and skill, I play the game.

Who am I, with rising fame?

Answers:

1.   Kevin De Bruyne: A pivotal figure at Manchester City, De Bruyne's exceptional playmaking abilities and vision have been crucial in the team's midfield.

2.   Mykhailo Mudryk: Known for his speed and technical ability, Mudryk shines as a dynamic winger for Chelsea, bringing a burst of energy and skill to the Premier League.

3.   Phil Foden: A versatile player for both England and Manchester City, Foden has

gained recognition for his skillful play in various positions, making a significant impact both in the midfield and defence.

Printed in Great Britain
by Amazon